BUT I$

LEG/

FUNDRAISING AND THE LAW

Sally Capper read law at Nottingham
University, and was called to the Bar in 1970.
She practised as a barrister for 7 years,
specialising in family law and landlord and
tenant law, before leaving the Bar to have
children.

She was Voluntary Legal Advisor to
Twickenham Citizens Advice Bureau for 10
years before joining Hounslow Law Centre
where she currently works. She is the
author of *Starting a Voluntary Group: the
legal choices.*

Sally Capper lives in Twickenham,
Middlesex with her husband, who is also a
barrister, and their two children.

BUT IS IT
LEGAL?

FUNDRAISING AND THE LAW

SALLY CAPPER

Bedford Square Press

Published by
BEDFORD SQUARE PRESS of the
National Council for Voluntary Organisations
26 Bedford Square, London WC1B 3HU

Typeset by Cylinder Typesetting Ltd, London
Printed and bound in England by
Dotesios Printers Ltd, Bradford-on-Avon

British Library Cataloguing in Publication Data

Capper, Sally
    But is it legal? : fundraising and the law.
    1. Great Britain. Fundraising. Law
    I. Title
    344.106'64

    ISBN 0-7199-1221-0

CONTENTS

Preface   vi

1 Introduction   1
Professional fundraisers   1
VAT and corporation tax   2

2 Collections   3
House-to-house collections   4
Street collections   5
Collecting boxes on premises   6

3 Lotteries and gaming   7
Exempt and non-commercial entertainments   8
Lotteries   9
Gaming   14

4 Running a bar   21
On club premises   22
At a fundraising function   23

5 Entertainments   25
Plays   26
Music and dancing   26
Film shows   27
Sporting contests and exhibitions   27

6 Fundraising with minors   29
Collections   30
Fêtes, bazaars etc   30
Lotteries   30
Gaming   30
Intoxicating liquor   30
Entertainments   31

7 Sponsored events   33
Car-boot sales   34

Appendix   35
Engaging a fundraising consultant or fundraiser

Further reading   38

Index   39

PREFACE

This book is intended for small groups who are considering various methods of raising funds. Its aim is to set out as simply and clearly as possible the law relating to each fundraising activity, and the steps you must take to stay within the law. Some of the law discussed, particularly that relating to lotteries and gaming, is very complex. Where this is so, only the more commonly arising situations are dealt with. If the project you are planning is not included it will probably be necessary for you to seek legal advice. Alternatively, you can consult the text of the relevant statutes referred to in connection with each subject, or refer to the specialist works listed on page 38.

Fundraisers of long standing may be surprised to discover on reading through the book that they have broken the law on a number of occasions. Why then is it necessary for them to understand and follow the various provisions of the law? First of all, it is important to realise that much of the legislation is directed to protecting generous members of the public from fraud. It is therefore helpful if genuine fundraisers do all they can to comply with the law. Secondly, any reported contravention of the law will discredit the fundraiser. Few groups can afford to run this risk. Lastly, many breaches of law in this field are criminal offences for which you can be charged, prosecuted, fined and even imprisoned.

1 INTRODUCTION

Fundraising for your favourite cause – whether a charity, a club or society, a pressure group or even the local hospital – can be an enjoyable and rewarding activity. But it can also be full of pitfalls for the unwary. There are laws that regulate many kinds of fundraising, including house-to-house and street collections, raffles, bingo or events where alcohol is sold. The provisions of those laws must, of course, be complied with and this book will help you find a way through the legal maze.

There is a also a general duty, in law, for individuals and groups to act in a manner which will not cause injury or offence to other people. If people or property are injured in the course of fundraising activities organised by you or by a group which you represent, you may be held liable for any damage done. It is therefore obviously very important both to take proper precautions to avoid any possible danger or annoyance to yourselves or to others and to insure against injuries and other unforeseen disasters. These can occur at even the best-regulated fundraising occasions, so you should inform your insurance company of any fundraising activity you are planning unless your group or society has a policy to cover you for a wide range of events involving the public. Remember too that if you hire a hall for fundraising you could be liable as occupiers for injuries caused by its poor or dangerous condition. It is easy to overlook the need for insurance cover where an event is to be held on premises other than your own.

This book is therefore designed as an introduction to the legislation covering the most usual types of fundraising activity. The information is applicable to England and Wales only. It should help you keep safely within the law, and protect you from making dangerous or expensive mistakes. Nevertheless, if you are planning a particularly unusual or novel fundraising

event and are not sure of how the law will affect you, then it would be sensible to seek specialist legal advice. As a general rule, if you are at all uncertain about the legality of any fundraising activity you are involved in, then ask your nearest law centre or your solicitor for expert advice. If your fundraising project involves games of chance, the sale of alcohol, or activities taking place upon the public highway, then the police might also be able to advise you.

Particular problems can arise if your fundraising activities involve employing a professional fundraiser or organising events for children. Both these aspects of fundraising are discussed in this book. If you are in any doubt as to your responsibilities towards the children taking part in any of your fundraising activities, then play safe and seek specialist legal advice.

Volunteer fundraisers collect millions of pounds every year to help good causes. With careful planning, and with the aid of the advice contained in this book, you can make sure that your fundraising activities are not only profitable and enjoyable, but also stay on the right side of the law.

Professional fundraisers

There is no law prohibiting a voluntary group from employing a professional fundraiser on a commercial basis. Some legislation does, however, indirectly discourage the profit motive in voluntary fundraising. For example, if you employ a professional fundraiser you may be refused a licence to collect from house to house. Licences for such collections can also be revoked (see page 4) on the grounds that insufficient of the proceeds is going to be devoted to charitable purposes, or that excessive remuneration is being retained by the professional.

Your concern, as a voluntary group, should be to exercise caution so far as employing anyone to help you to raise funds is concerned. Professional fundraising can readily attract the dishonest and unscrupulous, or lead to excesses of zeal with which you might not wish to be associated. If you do decide to employ a professional fundraiser you should, therefore, not only check all their references in full but also consider the terms of their employment very carefully. Decide exactly what you wish the fundraiser's duties and responsibilities to be, and on the amount of money you can afford to pay them, before committing yourself to any formal offer of employment. It is strongly recommended that any agreement with a professional fundraiser should be by written contract drawn up with the benefit of legal advice. Earlier correspondence while you are reaching agreement should be marked 'Subject to contract' to leave no room for doubt. You can obtain copies of a model contract for employing professional fundraisers from:
The Institute of Charity Fundraising
   Managers
208 Market Towers
London SW8 5NQ
Telephone: 01-627 3436
For further information about malpractice in fundraising see the NCVO report listed in Further reading on page 38.

If at all possible, you should arrange to pay a professional on a time-and-expenses basis. Payment by commission has in the past been associated with malpractice, and could give rise to legal difficulties if those making donations are not aware that a proportion of their gift, or of the total proceeds of the appeal, will be going to the fundraiser.

Whatever method of calculating payment is agreed, you should ensure that all money comes first to the voluntary group, that is that all cheques are made payable to it and all cash is paid into its bank account. Two further cautions: if the fundraising is to be a joint venture between two or more organisations or between your group and a professional fundraiser, do not overlook the possibility of the venture being unsuccessful or the professional becoming insolvent. And if there are to be large expenses involved in fundraising, there may well be good reasons to reconsider the project, or to insist on proper provision being made to insure against any loss if the funds raised do not match your expectations.

VAT and corporation tax

Profits from fundraising may not be exempt from taxation even for registered charities. They could constitute 'business activities' requiring registration for VAT if turnover is above the statutory limit, or they could constitute 'trade' making them liable for corporation tax. There are concessions, however, in the latter case for occasional charitable events. Professional advice should be sought, particularly if fundraising such as lotteries are undertaken on a regular basis.

2
COLLECTIONS

Perhaps the most obvious way to raise funds is to knock on people's doors and ask for them. Fundraising of this kind is dealt with by the *House-to-House Collections Act 1939* which controls house-to-house collections for charitable purposes. Note that 'charitable purposes' means *any charitable benevolent or philanthropic* purpose whether or not such purpose is charitable within the meaning of the law. This means that the Act is concerned with charity as the general public sees it, and not restricted to the narrower confines of the law where charity has a special meaning.

Before you can promote a collection (i.e. cause other people to act as collectors) you need either a licence, a police certificate or exemption from the Home Office. Any promoter or collector who acts without such necessary authority is guilty of an offence. It is important to note that the definition of 'collection' includes the sale of things so that the sale of programmes, raffle tickets, tombola tickets from house to house is within the general prohibition even where as in a society's lottery (see page 10) you are entitled to sell to members of the public. 'House' includes a place of business so that office collections are also prohibited without the necessary authorisation.

Home Office exemption

Exemption from the need to obtain a licence can be granted by the Home Office to a person pursuing a charitable purpose throughout the whole of England or a substantial part of it, who wishes to promote collections for that purpose. This is obviously not of relevance to most small groups but worth mentioning by way of explanation in case your group is part of a larger nationwide charity which has been so exempted. Such exemption has effect just as if a licence has been granted so that if you are collecting on the basis of a Home Office exemption you will be bound by the *House to House Collections Regulations 1947* (see page 5).

Police certificates

The chief officer of police for an area has power to grant a certificate to the person principally concerned in a collection, where he is satisfied that it is to be made within the locality and to be completed in a short time. If collection is made within the area and the period specified in the certificate, no licence will be necessary. This can be a very useful way for a small local group to arrange a collection or sell fête programmes etc. since promoters or collectors with the authority of a police certificate are not bound by the restrictions of the *House to House Collections Regulations 1947* (see page 5), and so will not need the expense of prescribed badges, collecting boxes etc.

If you apply to the police for a certificate in the Metropolitan Police District it is important to make it quite clear that you require a certificate and not a licence, since the police in London also deal with licence applications.

Licence

For house-to-house collections that do not fall within the categories above, the promoter (that is the person who causes others to act as collectors) will require a licence. This can be obtained from the licensing authorities who are:
1. In the City of London – the Common Council
2. Metropolitan Police District – the Commissioner of Police
3. Any other district – the district council. Applications are made in the prescribed form (obtainable from the licensing authority) and must be made not later than the first day of the month before it is intended to commence collection, although there is power to relax this for good reason.

Before undertaking or planning a house-to-house collection it is worth enquiring about the local practice on granting licences and certainly advisable to apply for a licence a good deal earlier than two months before it is intended to begin the collection.

Licences may be granted for periods of

4

not longer than twelve months. They can be refused (or if granted can be revoked) on a number of grounds namely:

1. If it appears that the total to be applied for charitable purposes is inadequate in proportion to the value of the proceeds.
2. That excessive remuneration is or is likely to be retained.
3. That granting a licence would be likely to facilitate offences under the Vagrancy Acts.
4. That the applicant has been convicted of certain offences involving dishonesty.
5. That the applicant has not been diligent to see collectors were fit and proper persons or to ensure that badges and certificates of authority did not go astray.
6. That the applicant or holder of the licence has refused or neglected to provide information reasonably required by the licensing authority.

The rules of practice that the promoter and collector must follow are found in the *House to House Collections Regulations 1947*.

Duties of the promoter

1. The promoter has to exercise all due diligence to ensure that fit and proper persons are chosen as collectors – they may not be under 16.
2. The promotor must give each collector
   (a) a certificate of authority
   (b) a prescribed badge
   (c) a collecting box or a receipt book clearly marked with the purposes of the collection.
Each collecting box or receipt book must have a distinguishing number. The promoter must keep a list of collectors' names and addresses and their corresponding numbers.
3. The promoter must exercise all due diligence to ensure that all certificates of authority and prescribed badges are destroyed when requested.
4. The promoter must ensure that collecting boxes are examined and opened in the presence of a responsible person other than himself and the amounts collected matched to the distinguishing numbers and

entered on the list. A similar course needs to be taken where there are receipt books.

Alternatively the unopened boxes may be returned to a bank and opened by a bank official alone.

5. Within one month of expiry of the licence an account of the collection must be furnished.

The accounts must be in the prescribed form and accompanied by the lists of collectors (see 2), vouchers for every item of expense and where relevant, receipt books.

It is an offence to furnish information in respect of a collection that is false in any material particular.

Duties of the collector

1. The collector must sign his certificate of authority and his badge. He must produce the certificate of authority on demand, wear his badge and return both to the promoter when the collection is completed or on demand of the promoter.

A police constable may require the collector to sign his name (to see if it corresponds with the signatures on the badge and certificate of authority).
2. Money must be received only by permitting the donor to place it in a collecting box himself – or by filling in a receipt and counterfoil in indelible pen or pencil signing the receipt and giving it to the donor.

Boxes must be returned to the promoter with the seal unbroken or receipt books returned with the corresponding money.
3. A collector must not 'importune to the annoyance of people', i.e. pester them nor stay once requested to leave.

Street collections

The law applicable to collecting in the street varies from area to area. Section 5 of the *Police Factories (Miscellaneous Provisions) Act 1916* gave power to local authorities to regulate street collections.

Where regulations have been made under this Act they set out the places and where and the conditions under which persons may be permitted in any street or public place within the area in question to collect money or sell articles for the benefit of charitable or other purposes. Regulations under the act do not apply where articles are sold in the ordinary course of trade for the purpose of earning a livelihood – or where no representation is made by or on behalf of the seller that any proceeds of sale will be devoted to any charitable purpose. Anyone acting in contravention of such regulations is guilty of an offence.

The authorities empowered to make regulations under the Act are:
1. The Common Council for the City of London
2. The Police Authority for the Metropolitan District (i.e. the Home Office)
3. District councils
In London (excluding the City of London) the current regulations are *Street Collection (Metropolitan Police District) Regulations 1979*. These are set out in Vol. 40 *Halsbury's Laws of England* 4th edition, para 470 (generally available in reference libraries). Applications for permits or certificates (the latter are for street collections where Christmas carols are sung or played) are made to the Metropolitan Police by the promoter of the collection. In other areas application for permits and enquires about regulations (most areas will have made such regulations) should be made to the district council.

You should make your enquiries and applications well in advance (probably at least a year) of your planned date for a street collection. Research has revealed that some authorities are very restrictive indeed in their willingness to grant permits for street collections. The regulations are likely to contain details of how to obtain a permit, rules regulating the collection, e.g. distances between collectors, not to annoy or inconvenience the public and similar rules as to numbered and sealed collecting boxes as found in the *House-to-House Collections Act 1939*. There may be special rules for Christmas carol collections and processions.

Collecting boxes on premises

There are no regulations for stationary collecting boxes, statuettes etc. Clearly you will need permission to place them on anyone's property and as a matter of commonsense they should be sealed and regularly emptied.

3
LOTTERIES AND GAMING

Lotteries

A lottery is a distribution of prizes by chance in which the participant pays for his chance (even if such payment includes some other benefit, for example entry to a fête, lucky programme, etc).

Lotteries are unlawful except within the terms provided by the *Lotteries and Amusements Act 1976*. A lottery may also be gaming (see below) and, if it is, the governing statute is the *Gaming Act 1968*.

Gaming

Gaming is the playing of a 'game of chance' for money or money's worth whether the person playing the game risks losing money or money's worth or not. 'Game of chance' includes a game of chance and skill combined. The law of gaming is covered by the *Gaming Act 1968.*

The distinction can be made between the simple lottery which is essentially a passive affair and gaming, e.g. bingo, in which the person concerned could be considered a 'player'.

> **Exempt and non-commercial entertainments**

– or What you can do at the garden fête

The law makes special provision for lotteries and gaming that take place at bazaars, fêtes, dinners, etc run for non-commercial purposes. For convenience these are dealt with together here, although the relevant law is not all in one place but found in the *Lotteries and Amusements Act 1976*, s. 3 and s. 15, and the *Gaming Act 1968*, s. 33 (as amended).

The law allows small lotteries (raffles, tombolas), gaming (bingo, roll a penny, etc) and gaming machines at functions that fall within the following definition:

> 'a bazaar, sale of work, fête, dinner dance, sporting or athletic event or other entertainment of similar character whether limited to one day or extending over two or more days'.

The whole proceeds of the entertainment (after permitted expenses) must be devoted to purposes *other than private gain.*

However, where the entertainment is run on behalf of a society which is established or conducted either:

1. wholly for purposes other than purposes of any commercial undertaking

or

2. wholly or mainly for the purpose of participation in or support of athletic sports or athletic games

then any proceeds 'applied for any purposes calculated to benefit the society as a whole shall not be held to be applied for purposes of private gain by reason only that their application for that purpose results in benefit to any person as an individual'.

This allows, for example, a music society to purchase instruments with the proceeds of the entertainment (or a football club their football kit) notwithstanding that individuals also benefit from such purchases.

Small lotteries

Section 3 of the *Lotteries and Amusements Act 1976* provides for the holding of small lotteries at an exempt entertainment (i.e. one within the definition above). This is the provision that allows raffles etc at fundraising functions usually for donated prizes. There is no need to apply to or notify anyone providing you keep the following rules:

1. The only expenses that can be deducted in connection with the lottery are:

> (a) The expenses of printing the lottery tickets.
>
> (In practice ready-printed cloakroom tickets can be purchased at a stationery shop for this kind of lottery since there are no special printing requirements.)
>
> (b) The expenses incurred in purchasing the prizes. The sum expended on prizes must not be more than £50.

2. None of the prizes may be cash prizes.
3. The sale and issue of tickets or chances in the lottery and the announcement of results *must* take place on the premises where the entertainment takes place and during its

progress. (So that if you sell tickets in a small lottery from door to door you are committing an offence both under *Lotteries and Amusements Act 1976* and under the *House- to-House Collections Act 1939*.)

4. The opportunity to take part in the lottery or other gaming must not be the only or substantial inducement of persons to attend the entertainment.

N.B. These rules are applicable to small lotteries only. Much of the confusion that arises from the law of lotteries comes from assuming there is one set of rules. There are in fact three (four including local authority lotteries) different sets of rules, each set only applicable to its respective kind of lottery – see pages 10-14 for other kinds of lottery.

Amusements with prizes

Section 15 of the *Lotteries and Amusements Act 1976* makes provision for amusements with prizes that constitute lotteries or gaming or both at an exempt entertainment. This is the provision that allows roll a penny, wheel of fortune, bingo, etc at fundraising functions.

Once again, the whole proceeds of the entertainment must be devoted to purposes other than private gain, and the opportunities to win prizes at amusements together with any other facilities for participating in lotteries or gaming must not be the only or only substantial inducement to attend the entertainment. The latter requirement makes it clear that an 'all-gambling' garden fête would take the organisers outside the special rules for such entertainments – you are expected to have the usual cake stalls, secondhand books, etc in addition to provision for lotteries and gaming.

Prizes under s. 15 may be in cash or in kind and no limit is placed on stakes or prizes.

Note however that if the entertainment is to take place on premises licensed or registered for gaming (see page 14) you cannot rely on s. 15 but are restricted to your usual conditions.

Where any equipment is hired for running an 'amusement with prizes' at an exempt entertainment, it should be by way of an hire charge agreed before the entertainment. Hire charges calculated on the amount of takings or use to which the equipment is put will be held to be an application of the proceeds for the purposes of private gain and cannot be claimed as expenses of the entertainment.

Gaming machines

If your entertainment falls within the definition of an exempt entertainment then by virtue of s. 33 of the *Gaming Act 1968* (as amended) you may provide gaming machines for those attending. The Gaming Act uses the expression 'non-commercial entertainment' but defines it in exactly the same terms as the exempt entertainment of the *Lotteries and Amusements Act*. There is no restriction as yet on the kind of gaming machine which can be used although there is power under the Act for further regulations to be made by the Secretary of State.

Remember that once again

1. The whole proceeds of the entertainment must be devoted to purposes other than private gain.

2. The opportunity to win prizes by means of the machine or that opportunity together with other facilities for lotteries and gaming must not be the only inducement to attend the entertainment.

Payment for hire of the machines should be by way of hire charge only. Any method of payment based on the amount of takings or the amount of use to which the equipment is put will be held to be an application of the proceeds for the purpose of private gain and cannot be claimed as expenses of the entertainment.

Entertainments on premises registered or licensed for gaming may not take advantage of s. 33 but are restricted to their usual conditions.

Lotteries

There are three kinds of lottery permitted under the *Lotteries and Amusements Act*

1976 (excluding local authority lotteries which are not dealt with here): small lotteries, private lotteries and societies' lotteries. Each type of lottery has its own rules – the fundraiser must make a choice and comply with the rules for the type of lottery chosen. Anyone involved in any way with an unlawful lottery risks committing a criminal offence. Section 2 of the *Lotteries and Amusements Act* casts its net very wide, so that it it not only the promoter but, for example, the printer, publisher of an advertisement of the lottery or lists of the prizewinners etc. who is guilty of an offence.

Small lotteries

These are lotteries permitted at an exempt entertainment and are dealt with in full above.

Private lotteries

Whereas small lotteries are limited by the place where you may sell the lottery tickets (at an exempt entertainment), private lotteries are limited by the persons to whom you may sell the tickets. One of a group of people who live on the same premises or work on the same premises may promote a lottery and sell tickets to his or her fellows living or working there. This is the provision that permits the office sweepstake. However in this case the whole proceeds of the lottery (after stationery expenses etc) must be paid out in prizes so it cannot be used as a means of raising funds.

However, in addition, any member of a society authorised in writing by the governing body of that society may promote a lottery, and tickets may be sold to members of that society. Where a member of a society promotes a private lottery the proceeds (after expenses) may be devoted to the provision of prizes or the purposes of the society (e.g. where prizes are donated) or both. This gives scope for a society member to promote a lottery to raise funds for the society.

N.B. The society must be established for purposes not connected with betting, gaming or lotteries – so it is not within the law to form a society to raise money by running a lottery even if it is intended to use the proceeds for charitable purposes.

The following rules apply:

1. No written notice or advertisement or the lottery may be exhibited save on the premises of the society for whose members the lottery is promoted.
2. The price of every ticket must be the same and the price must be on the ticket.
3. Every ticket must bear on its face the names and addresses of the promoters, a statement of the persons to whom the sale of the tickets is restricted and a statement that no prize will be delivered to any person other than the person to whom the winning ticket was sold by the promoters.
4. There can be no free tickets, discounting or refunds.
5. No ticket can be sent by post.

Although a private lottery run by a society is limited by the size of its membership it is not limited in other ways, e.g. as to the price of a ticket or the size of the prizes. Prizes may be in cash or kind.

Societies' lotteries

The advantage of running a lottery as a society's lottery is that the sale of tickets is not restricted by place (as in a small lottery) or by person (as in a private lottery). Tickets may be sold to members of the public at large and this widens the fundraising possibilities enormously.

However, a society's lottery is not something to arrange in a hurry. As well as the cost of printing the tickets, there is the cost of the registration fee (see page 11) to recover. Moreover the fundraiser will be faced with the rather daunting regulations applicable to such lotteries. In practice these involve making sure that the intended lottery will fall within the regulations, plus a certain amount of not too arduous paperwork – well worth the effort if someone is prepared to take the trouble. Incidentally there is no reason at all why tickets for a society's lottery cannot be sold and the draw made at an entertainment such as bazaar, fête, etc. Prior sales of the tickets greatly boost the profits in comparison with the small lottery (see page

8) which is usually organised at such events.

A society's lottery is a lottery promoted on behalf of a society which is established and conducted wholly or mainly for one or more of the following purposes:
1. charitable purposes
2. participation in or support of athletic sports or games or cultural activities
3. purposes not within (1) or (2) but which are neither purposes of private gain nor purposes of any commercial undertaking Most voluntary societies will fall within this clause. Note too that purposes which benefit an individual are not held to be purposes of private gain if they are calculated to benefit the society as a whole, so that the purchase, for example, of instruments for members of a music society would not be held to be purposes of private gain notwithstanding that individuals have benefited from them.

Before a society's lottery is lawful the society must be *registered* with the local authority and, if the total value of tickets is in excess of £10,000, also with the Gaming Board. In addition it must be promoted in accordance with a *scheme* approved by the society. The promotion of societies' lotteries is limited to Great Britain.

The scheme

The *Schedule* to the *Lotteries Regulations* 1977 sets out what a lottery scheme should contain. In practice if you enquire about societies' lotteries your local authority may provide you with a model scheme so that it is merely a question of deciding with fellow members how to fill in the form. The scheme must be approved by the society – it is *not* sufficient for the society merely to agree that a lottery or raffle should be held, it must approve the whole scheme. If lotteries are to be run with sales of tickets in excess of £10,000 the scheme must also be approved by the Gaming Board.

Societies' lottery schemes must specify:
1. The name and address of the society by whom the scheme was approved.
2. (a) The name and address of the registration authority.
   (b) The date of registration.

(c) The reference number (if any) of registration.
3. The period during which it is to have effect (not more than three years).
4. The number of lotteries allowed in any 12-month period (not more than 52).
5. The proportion of proceeds (not exceeding one half) which may be appropriated for prizes and that this shall not be exceeded (save exceptionally where proceeds fall short of the sum reasonably estimated and the appropriation is necessary to fulfil an unconditional undertaking as to prizes).

Registration

Application for registration of a society's lottery should be made to:
1. the district council
2. the Common Council of the City of London
3. a London borough council
If there is doubt as to which district the society is in, application should be made to the council within whose area the society's head office is situated. The current fee for registration (1988) is £25. A further £12.50 renewal fee is payable on 1 January of each year.

An application for registration must specify the purposes for which the society is established and conducted. (If your society has a formal constitution or rules you can simply quote the clause or rule setting out the objects of the society.) Registration may be refused or revoked on the basis that the purposes for which the society is established and conducted are not within those specified above (i.e. charitable purposes etc.) or that any person (N.B. not just the promoter) has been convicted of an offence under the *Lotteries and Amusements Act 1976*, or the *Betting, Gaming and Lotteries Act 1963*, or an offence involving fraud and dishonesty in connection with a lottery promoted or proposed to be promoted on behalf of the society. There is an appeal to the Crown Court against refusal or revocation of registration.

The following rules apply to societies'

lotteries: (see s. 11 of the *Lotteries and Amusements Act 1976, Lotteries Regulations 1977, Lotteries (Amendment) Regulations 1981*).

1. The promoter must be a member of the society and authorised in writing to act as such.

2. Every ticket and every notice or advertisement must specify the society's name, the name and address of the promoter and the date of the lottery.

The date of the lottery is usually that on which a draw takes place *but* in the case of an instant lottery (e.g. of the scratch-and-see type) the date specified is the last date on which tickets are to be on sale unless there is an additional draw for a major prize in which case that is the date to be specified.

The ticket must specify the name of the registration authority with which the society is registered.

3. The whole proceeds of a lottery after deducting sums lawfully used to pay expenses and provide prizes must be applied to the purposes of the society.

4. The amount appropriated to prizes must not exceed half the whole proceeds and the amount appropriated on account of expenses must not exceed the expenses actually incurred or 25 per cent of the proceeds, whichever is the less (save exceptionally where proceeds fall short of the sum reasonably estimated. Different rules about expenses apply where the scheme is registered with the Gaming Board – see page 13.)

5. No ticket or chance may be sold at a price exceeding 50p.

6. The price of every ticket or chance must be the same and must be stated on the ticket. There must be no free tickets or refunding of ticket money (e.g. for ticket sellers).

7. No prize may exceed £2,000 in amount or value. (Different rules apply where the scheme is registered with the Gaming Board – see page 13.)

8. No ticket or chance may be sold to a person in any street – save in a kiosk or shop premises which has no space for the accommodation of customers.

9. No ticket may be sold in:
   (a) a licensed betting office
   (b) any premises used wholly or mainly for providing amusements with prizes or slot machines or both
   (c) in any bingo or gaming club (for which a licence under the *Gaming Act 1968* is in force).

10. No ticket may be sold in a vending machine.

11. No ticket or chance may be sold by a person when visiting any other at his home in the discharge of any official, professional or commercial function not connected with lotteries.

12. No ticket or chance may be sold, distributed or offered for sale more than three months before the date of any previous society's lottery promoted on behalf of the same society.

13. Where information appearing on a ticket or advertisement includes a reference to a person involved in promoting a lottery for reward, the size of the lettering used must be no bigger than the size of the smallest lettering used to name the society, and the reference to the promoter must not be given greater prominence than the name of the society.

14. Persons supplying lottery tickets for use in 'instant lotteries' must not be asked to supply tickets which are identifiable as winning tickets prior to sale (i.e. even the promoter must not know).

15. No prize may be offered on such terms that the winning of the prize depends upon the purchase of more than one ticket or chance.

16. No society shall hold more than 52 lotteries in any period of 12 months (but when the date of two or more society's lotteries promoted on behalf of one society is the same and the total value of tickets does not exced £20,000 all those lotteries shall be treated as one).

17. The date of any lottery promoted on behalf of a society shall not be less than seven days after the date of any previous lottery promoted on behalf of that society except that the date of a lottery promoted

for the purpose of selling tickets or chances wholly or mainly to persons attending a particular athletic or sporting event may be less than seven days after the date of a previous lottery promoted on behalf of the society. (This covers the situation where for example there are two home fixtures for a football club within one week.)

Lotteries under schemes registered with the Gaming Board

Where the total value of tickets or chances exceed £10,000 registration with the Gaming Board is necessary.

The Board must register a scheme unless
1. The society has not registered with the local authority.
2. The scheme is contrary to law.
3. The Board is not satisfied
    (a) that all lotteries promoted by or on behalf of the applicant during the preceding five years have been properly conducted
    (b) that all fees payable have been paid
    (c) that accounts and other information required by the Gaming Board have been submitted.
4. It appears to the Board that an unsuitable person will be a paid employee in connection with promoting a lottery under the scheme (an unsuitable person in this context is one who has been convicted of certain listed offences or an offence involving fraud or dishonesty).

The Gaming Board's power of refusal is subject to the overriding direction of the Home Secretary. A registration fee determined by the Gaming Board is payable to them and in addition a further fee is payable for each lottery promoted under the scheme.

Lotteries promoted under the scheme which are required to be registered with the Board are divided into:
1. Short-term lotteries: those held less than one month after the date of a previous lottery. Here the maximum value of tickets sold is £30,000 and the maximum value of any prize is £3,000.
2. Medium-term lotteries: those held between one and three months after the date of a previous lottery. The maximum value of tickets sold shall be £60,000 and the maximum value of any prize shall be £4,500.
3. Any other lotteries: those held over three months after the date of a previous lottery. The maximum value of tickets sold shall be £120,000 and the maximum prize £6,000.

Where the proceeds of a lottery exceed £10,000 the amount appropriated on account of expenses (exclusive of prizes) must not exceed whichever is the less of the expenses actually incurred or 15 per cent of those proceeds or such larger percentage not exceeding 25 per cent as the Gaming Board may authorise.

Returns

The promoter of a society's lottery (other than those registered with the Gaming Board) must send a return to the local authority not later than the end of the third month after the date of the lottery. Normally the local authority will provide return forms for a society registered with them. Such returns must include:
1. a copy of the scheme under which the lottery was promoted
2. details of the whole proceeds of the lottery
3. the sums taken from those proceeds on account of prizes and expenses
4. the purpose to which proceeds of the lottery were applied
5. the date of the lottery

Returns must be certified by two members of the society other than the promoter, being persons of full age appointed in writing by the governing body of the society.

The promoters of schemes registered with the Gaming Board must submit accounts to them on forms they provide.

Fundraisers may find the following checklist useful:

Checklist for printing requirements for a society's lottery tickets
1. The name of the society.
2. The name and address of the promoter (N.B. remember the restrictions on lettering

size if promotion is for reward – see page 12).
3. The date of the lottery.
4. The price of the ticket.
5. The name of the registration authority with which the society is registered.
6. Details of the prizes. N.B. this is in fact *not* a requirement but naturally usually included to attract purchases of tickets. If there is any doubt as to the availablity of a prize it should *not* be included. Terms such as 'major prize to be confirmed' or 'additional prizes to be announced' can get over this difficulty.

Gaming

The *Gaming Act 1968* imposes tight restrictions on gaming to prevent exploitation for commercial purposes. It then lifts the general restrictions to a greater or lesser degree to permit gaming of certain kinds in certain clearly defined circumstances. These can be divided into:
1. Gaming (other than gaming by machine) permitted without the need for registration or licensing of premises.
2. Registration or licensing of premises under Part II of the Act.
3. Gaming machines.

The general rules
Part I of the *Gaming Act 1968* sets out the general prohibitory rules.
1. The playing of games which involve playing or staking against a bank (these are known as bankers games) and games of unequal chance are prohibited except on domestic occasions in a private dwelling, hostel or hall of residence, i.e. roulette, baccarat, chemin de fer, blackjack, pontoon etc are in general prohibited.
2. There can be no charge made for taking part in gaming save
   (a) an entrance subscription or annual subscription or quarterly or half-yearly instalment or an annual subscription to a club providing it is not a temporary club

or a subscription paid for temporary membership.
   (b) such small charges permitted under s.40 (see below).
3. There can be no levy on stakes or winnings.
4. Gaming in any street or public place is prohibited. (There are exceptions for dominoes and cribbage in public houses and liquor licensing justices may authorise certain other games.)
5. Any person under 18 is prohibited from taking part in gaming on premises in respect of which a justice's licence is in force.

If gaming takes place in contravention of these rules every person concerned in the organisation and management of the gaming is guilty of an offence.

Gaming (other than gaming by machine) permitted without the need for registration or licensing of premises
Small voluntary organisations may find these provisions sufficient for their fund-raising needs. Providing they keep within the rules they do not have to take any action or seek any permission to organise gaming under these sections.

Amusements with prizes at fêtes, bazaars, etc
Section 15 of the *Lotteries and Amusements Act 1976* makes provision for gaming at certain non-commercial entertainments, fêtes, bazaars, etc (see page 8).

Bingo, bridge or whist drives in a club
Section 40 of the *Gaming Act 1968* allows equal chance gaming to be promoted by clubs and miners' welfare institutes without registration or licensing under Part II of the Act. (Although clubs which are registered or licensed may also take advantage of this section.) It is necessary to comply with the following conditions:
1. The club must have at least 25 members and not be of a temporary nature.
2. The gaming must be carried on as one of the club activities (i.e. not its sole activity).
3. Where the only gaming promoted on a

14

particular day (excluding gaming machines) is bridge or whist then the maximum charge is £6 per day. Otherwise (e.g. bingo) the maximum permitted charge is 25p per day. All stake money must be returned to the players as cash prizes (i.e. the fundraising element is in the entry charge).

4. Bankers' games may not be played.

5. Gaming must not be advertised to the public nor played on premises to which the public have access (i.e. gaming is for members only).

Bingo, bridge or whist drives at entertaiments not held for private gain

Section 41 in effect provides for fundraising bridge or whist drives or bingo sessions. There is no need to be a club to take advantage of this section. This section is *not* applicable to premises registered as licensed under the Act or to gaming by machine. It is necessary to comply with the following conditions:

1. Not more than one payment not exceeding £2 may be made (whether by entrance fee or stake) by each player.

2. The total value of all prizes must not exceed £200. (If there is a series of games e.g. a knock-on competition in which people have qualified on previous days, the prize limit for the final game is raised to £400.)

3. The whole proceeds after deductions for expenses must be applied for purposes other than private gain. N.B. If a society established or conducted for non-commercial purposes or wholly or mainly for participation in or support of athletic sports and games applies the proceeds of an entertainment for a purpose calculated to benefit the society, the proceeds are not to be taken as applied for private gain simply because they also benefit an individual, e.g. an amateur sports club may use proceeds to purchase kit for its members notwithstanding that this also is of benefit to individuals.

4. Expenses are limited to the reasonable cost of facilities.

5. Bankers' games are not allowed.

Registration of members' clubs

Members' clubs and miners' welfare institutes may register under Part II of the *Gaming Act 1968* and provide gaming on a less restricted basis than under the sections quoted above. A members' club is one managed by and on behalf of members and not for purposes of private gain. A miners' welfare institute is an association organised for the social well-being and recreation of persons employed in or around coal mines which is either managed in a manner specified by the 1968 Act or which has premises held on charitable trust.

Application for registration is made to the gaming licensing committee of the justices in the area in which the club is situated. An application form (to comply with Schedule 1 of the *Gaming Act (Registration under Part II) Regulations 1969)* may be available from the clerk to the licensing committee or alternatively could be purchased from a solicitors law stationers. The application is sent to the clerk to the licensing authority and then not later than 7 days after applying a copy must be sent to:

1. the chief officer of police for the area

2. the collector of Customs and Excise for the area

3. the Gaming Board of Great Britain, Berkshire House, 168-73 High Holborn, London WC1 7AA

It is obviously simpler to send the copies at the same time as the application is sent to ensure keeping the time requirements.

Not later than 14 days from making the application notice of application must be advertised in a newspaper circulating in the registration authority's area. (Again it is sensible to arrange this at the same time as making the application.) The notice must specify:

1. The applicant's name.

2. The name of the club.

3. The address of the premises which are to be registered.

It must contain nothing else except a statement that anyone who desires to object to the registration of the premises should send to the clerk to the licensing authority two copies of a brief statement in writing of the grounds of his objection by the date specified. This date must not be less than 14 days after the publication of the advertisement.

The applicant will be notified of the date, time and place of the hearing (at least 14 days after the date specified in the newspaper advertisement) and provided with a copy of any objections which have been made.

Registration is initially for one year. The applicant may then apply for renewal after five months but not later than two months before the date on which the registration is due to expire (although there is provision for late application if the registration authority consider the delay was due to inadvertence). On renewal (on the basis that the club will have established its bona fides) the club or institute may ask and be granted re-registration for a period up to 10 years. The initial registration fee is £105 and the fee for renewal £54.

Grounds for refusal to register or to renew registration

The justice *must* refuse to register or renew registration of a club if it appears to them that:
1. It is not a bona fide members' club
2. It has less than 25 members
3. It is merely of a temporary character
4. It is established and conducted principally for gaming unless the gaming in question consists exclusively of playing bridge or whist or both.

The justices *may* refuse to register or renew registration where
1. The club has previously been registered but either its registration has been cancelled or renewal has been refused.
2. A person has been convicted of an offence under the Gaming Act 1968 in connection with the premises.
3. The premises have not been conducted in a way to prevent disturbance or disorder.
4. Gaming on the premises has been dishonestly conducted.
5. The premises have been used for unlawful purposes or as a resort of criminals or prostitutes. (If they have been habitually

so used renewal of registration must be refused.)
6. Any duty payable remains unpaid.

The registration authority may impose restrictions limiting gaming to a particular part or parts of the premises. There is an appeal to the Crown Court against the justices' refusal to register or renew the registration of a club.

The following rules apply to gaming on premises registerd under Part II of the *Gaming Act 1968.*
1. Only members of the club and their bona fide guests may take part in gaming. A member must have applied for or been nominated for membership at least 48 hours before he began to take part in the gaming. A person is not considered to be a bona fide guest if he is charged for admission or makes any payment in respect of gaming other than stakes hazarded or payment for losses incurred in the gaming.
2. No one may take part in gaming who is not on the premises when the gaming takes place there.
3. The charges made for gaming are limited to £2 per person per day and no levy on stakes or winnings may be made.
4. Bankers' games and games of unequal chance are only permitted if of a kind specified by regulations. The *Gaming Act (Registration under Part II Regulations) 1969* permits pontoon (other than blackjack or any form of pontoon where the right to hold the bank does not pass amongst the players) and chemin de fer on registered premises.
5. No persons under 18 (including a club employee) may be present in any room while gaming takes place. They may exceptionally be present where bingo is being played provided they do not play themselves.

If any of the above rules are contravened, every officer of the club or institute will be guilty of an offence. Similarly every person concerned in the organisation or management of the gaming will be guilty of an offence unless he or she proves the contravention occurred without their knowledge or they exercised all such care as was reasonable in the circumstances to ensure no contravention would take place.

If gaming is to be the principal purpose of the club, or bankers' games of a kind not permitted or registered but permitted on licensed premises are required, then the club will need to be licensed under Part II rather than registered. This is a more costly and complicated procedure and generally unsuitable for small voluntary groups. Accordingly it is not dealt with in this book.

Gaming machines

Part III of the *Gaming Act 1968* applies to machines which are:

> 'constructed and adapted for playing a game of chance by means of the machine and which have a slot or aperture for the insertion of money or money's worth in the form of cash or tokens'

The restrictions on gaming machines do not however apply to machines where all that can be won is another chance to play the game or the player's money back.

If you want to provide gaming machines you can do so in one of the following ways:
1. Incidental to a non-commercial entertainment.
2. By permit.
3. By registration under Part II or Part III of the *Gaming Act 1968*.

Gaming machines incidental to a non-commercial entertainment

Section 33 of the *Gaming Act 1968* (as amended) allows the provision of gaming machines at a bazaar, fête, etc (see pages 8-9).
N.B. A gaming machine licence is not required for gaming machines provided under this section nor is gaming machine duty payable.

Permits for gaming machines

There are two types of gaming machines: amusement-with-prizes machines which pay out very small winnings and jackpot machines which pay out substantial prizes.

To provide amusement-with-prizes machines the fundraiser must apply for a permit under s. 34 of the *Gaming Act 1968*. Application is made to the local authority in whose area the premises where it is intended to have the gaming machines are situated. The relevant local authorities are:
1. In the City of London – the Common Council
2. In Greater London – London borough
3. Outside London – district council
(Where gaming machines are provided in public houses, the liquor licensing justices are the licensing authority.)

It is possible for a local authority to make general resolutions restricting either the class of premises to which they will grant permits or the numbers of machines which they will allow when granting such permits – and so it is worth enquiring from the local authority whether any such resolutions have been passed before application is made. A permit may be granted or renewed for any period up to 3 years (in practice the 3-year period is usual). It may be granted subject to a condition limiting the number of machines. Application to renew should be made not less than one month before the existing permit is due to expire to avoid the permit expiring and the consequent need to put the machines out of use. A s. 34 permit cannot be operative where premises are registered or licensed under Part II of the *Gaming Act 1968*.

The following conditions apply to amusement-with-prizes machines:
1. The charge for one game must not be more than 10p.
2. In any one game the prize must be one only of the following:
   (a) a money prize not exceeding £2 or tokens exchangable to that amount
   (b) non-monetary prizes or tokens to a value of not more than £4
   (c) a combined value prize not exceeding £2 in cash plus a non-monetary prize not exceeding £4 less the amount of the money prize (i.e. the total value of the prize must not exceed £4)
   (d) one or more tokens which can be used for playing one or more further games or which can be exchanged for a

non-monetary prize within(b) above
(e) where a player wins a game and is
automatically given a further opportunity
to play he may receive one money prize
not exceeding £2 for all the games
played.

Gaming machines and registration under Part II or Part III Gaming Act 1968

If your club is registered under Part II of the
Gaming Act 1968 (see page 15), you may
provide two gaming machines of the
jackpot type on your premises, as well as
the other forms of gaming allowed, without
further application. If it is not so registered
you may choose to register instead under
Part III of the Act which is a slightly simpler
and cheaper process than registration
under Part II but authorises only gaming by
means of machine.

Application should be made to the
gaming licensing committee of the justices
for the area in which the premises are
situated. A copy of the application must be
sent to the chief officer of police for the area
not later than 7 days after the application is
made. (In practice it is safer to send the
copy at the same time as the application in
order to ensure that the time requirement is
met.)

A hearing will only be necessary if
objection is made to your application.
Registration under Part III is effective for
5 years but can be renewed for further
5-year periods. Application for renewal
(again with a copy sent to the police not later
than 7 days after the application is made)
should be made not earlier than 3 months
and not later than 6 weeks before the date
on which the registration is due to expire.
(There is provision for late applications if
the justices are satisfied that failure to apply
was due to inadvertence.)

The application *must* be refused if it
appears to the licensing authority that the
premises are wholly or mainly frequented
by persons under 18. It *may* be refused if it
appears that
1. The club is not a bona fide members'
club.
2. It has less than 25 members.

3. It is of a merely temporary character.
If any person has been convicted of
offences under the *Gaming Act 1968* or
regulations made under it in connection
with the premises in question. There is an
appeal to the Crown Court against refusal of
an application. The current fee (1988) for
registration under Part III is £54 and £27 for
renewal.

Use of gaming machines on registered premises

The following rules apply to the use of
gaming machines on premises registered
under Part II or Part III of the Act.
1. No more than two machines are allowed
on the premises.
2. The maximum charge for playing one
game must not exceed 20p.
3. All prizes must be in coin or coins.
4. There must be clearly indicated on every
machine the prizes offered, the description
of the circumstances in which these prizes
cannot be won (if there are any special
circumstances) and the percentage of pay
out.
5. The use of machines is prohibited
whenever the public have access to the
premises.

No limit is placed on the value of the prize
which can be paid out although there is
provision for the Home Secretary to
prescribe a maximum. At present by
agreement between the Gaming Board and
the industry the maximum jackpot has been
set at £100.

There is also provision for the Home
Secretary to make regulations imposing
special requirements in respect of
machines installed in registered premises
or requiring records or accounts to be sent
to the Gaming Board and to the police.
Gaming machines may only be emptied by
authorised persons. These are any officer or
member of the club or institute or their
employees. It is not lawful for the supplier to
empty gaming machines. A breach of any of
the conditions imposed by the *Gaming Act*
in respect of gaming machines makes every
officer of the club guilty of a criminal offence
unless he can prove that the breach

occurred without his knowledge and that he took reasonable care to prevent such breach.

Excise duty payable on gaming
Gaming machine licence duty
Except where gaming machines are provided at a non-commercial entertainment (see page 17) they require a gaming licence on which duty is payable (*Betting and Gaming Duties Act 1981*, s. 22).

Bingo duty
Under s. 17 of the *Betting and Gaming Duties Act 1981* a duty known as bingo duty is charged on the playing of bingo. If the value of prizes is kept below £400 a day or £1,000 a week however such duty is not chargeable. Full details of the requirements of the *Betting and Gaming Duties Act 1981* under these sections and the rates of duty chargeable may be obtained from local Customs and Excise offices or from H.M. Customs and Excise headquarters, Kings Beam House, Mark Lane, London EC3R 7HE.

If your club chooses to licence rather than register their premises for gaming, gaming licences duty will be payable on the licence unless it is restricted to bingo only.

4
RUNNING A BAR

The retail sale of alcohol normally requires a justices' licence. The position is different where a members' club run a bar. The members are taken to own jointly all the property of the club and this includes the club's supply of drink. Even though money changes hands, there will be no sale in law. Nevertheless section 39 of the *Licensing Act 1964* requires that no intoxicating liquor shall be supplied *on club premises* without either registration or a justices' licence.

What is the position of a club wanting to run a bar other than on club premises? If the club premises *are* registered for the supply of intoxicating liquor, then the club can supply it at other premises used for members on a 'special occasion'. Only members and their guests may be permitted access and the drink supplied must be consumed on the premises. If club premises are not registered it is not clear whether a bar can be run solely for members and their guests, in, for example, a hired hall although logic would suggest that this is not prohibited.

What is absolutely certain is that if a bar is run by anyone at a fundraising function that is open to members of the public, it must be authorised either by an occasional permission or by an occasional licence.

On club premises

Registration of a club
Although there is provision in the *Licensing Act 1964* for a members' club to obtain a justices licence – intoxicating liquor is usually provided under the authority of a registration certificate. To obtain registration the club must meet the following conditions:
1. The club rules must require an interval of at least two days before a person can become a member or make use of his rights of membership.
2. The club must be conducted in good faith and have not less than 25 members.
3. Intoxicating liquor is to be supplied to members on the premises only by and on behalf of the club.

4. The purchase and supply of the liquor is to be managed by an elective committee. (An elective committee is defined in Schedule 7 of the *Licensing Act 1964.*)
5. No arrangements are to be made for anyone to receive financial benefit (e.g. by way of commission) from the supply of intoxicating liquor.

In deciding the question of good faith magistrates may have regard to:
1. Any arrangement restricting the purchase of intoxicating liquor (e.g. ties to any manufacturer or supplier).
2. Any provision whereby the profit can be applied other than for the benefit of the club or for charitable, benevolent or political purposes.
3. The arrangements for providing members with information as to the finances of the club.
4. The nature of the premises.
The details required in the application are set out in Schedule 5 of the *Licensing Act 1964* although the licensing justices clerk will normally provide forms. Objections to the issue or renewal of a certificate may be made by:
1. the chief officer of police
2. the local authority
3. the fire authority
4. by any person affected by reason of his occupation of or interest in other premises.
This is on the basis that:
1. The application is defective, i.e. not in accordance with the Act, or inaccurate.
2. The premises are unsuitable.
3. The necessary conditions have not been satisfied.
4. The club is conducted in a disorderly manner or for an unlawful purpose or the club rules habitually disregarded.
5. The club premises are habitually used for an unlawful purpose, indecent displays, are the resort of criminals or prostitutes, or there is frequent drunkenness or within the preceding 12 months there have been illegal sales or persons not qualified to be supplied have habitually been admitted for that purpose.
6. The premises were formerly licensed but have been disqualified by order of the

court.
There is provision for the local authority (and the fire authority if this is not the local authority) to inspect the premises before they are first registered.

The supply of intoxicating liquor in a registered club

The hours during which drink can be supplied will be those fixed by the club. They must however comply with the following conditions:
1. The hours fixed must not be longer than the general licensing hours for the district.
2. The hours fixed must not start earlier or end later than the general licensing hours for the district.
3. There must be a break of at least two hours in the afternoon.
4. On Sunday, Christmas Day and Good Friday the afternoon break must include the hours from 3 until 5 and there may not be more than three and a half hours after 5.
The club chairman or secretary must notify the clerk to the justices in writing of the hours permitted by club rules and no changes to these hours can be effective until they have been similarly notified.

Once a club is registered it may supply drink in accordance with its rules on the following basis:
1. To members and their guests for consumption on the premises.
2. To a member in person for consumption off the premises. This is restricted to supplying on club premises, i.e. where the registered club is supplying drink on a special occasion at a different place the supply for consumption off the premises will not be permitted even to a member in person.
3. To non-members for consumption on the premises. Even though in this situation it will amount to a sale, a licence will not be necessary. However at the time of issuing or renewing a registration certificate the justices will consider the club rules and may attach conditions restricting the sale of liquor on the premises (i.e. to non-members). The justices are restricted however in making such conditions and

may not make conditions prohibiting the sale to the members of other clubs in certain circumstances, for example to a local club whose premises are temporarily closed or a club of a similar nature.

At a fundraising function

Occasional permissions

If you intend to have a bar at a fundraising function it it obviously more profitable to run it yourselves. To do this you will need an occasional permission. The *Licensing (Occasional Permissions) Act 1983* allows the licensing justices to grant to an officer of an eligible organisation an occasional permission authorising the sale of intoxicating liquor for a period not exceeding 24 hours. No more than four such permissions may be granted to the same organisation in any 12 months.

The application should be made in writing (the clerk to the licensing justices will normally provide a form if requested). The application requires the following details:
1. The name and address of the applicant and his date and place of birth
2. The name of the organisation and its purpose
3. The nature of the applicant's office (chairman, secretary, etc.)
4. The date amd place and nature of the function
5. The kinds of intoxicating liquor to be sold
6. Details of any occasional permissions granted to the organisation in the preceding 12 months

To be 'eligible' an organisation must not be carried on for private gain although a purpose calculated to benefit a non-commercial undertaking as a whole shall not be taken to be a purpose of private gain merely because it results in benefit to an individual. (For example, an organisation run to purchase aids and equipment for the handicapped would be 'eligible' even though individuals benefit from the purchases.)

Two copies of the application must be served on the licensing justices not less than one month before the date of the function for which the occasional permission is required. In practice it is *very important* to apply much earlier than one month before the date of the function. The application will be dealt with at the next licensing sessions, unless these are to be held within the next fifteen days in which case it will be heard at the next but one sessions. If you do not allow a wide time margin you may find there is no licensing session to hear your application before the date planned for your function.

A fee, currently £4, is payable for each grant. This may include more than one permission granted at the same time.

The justices must be satisfied that:

1. The officer is a fit and proper person to sell intoxicating liquor and is resident in their licensing district.

2. The place where the function is to be held will be suitable for the sale of intoxicating liquor and is in their licensing district.

3. The sale of intoxicating liquor at the function is not likely to result in disturbance or annoyance being caused to residents in the neighbourhood or in any disorderly conduct.

The occasional permission will specify the place, the kinds of liquor to be sold and the hours approved.

Occasional licences

If you do not intend running the bar yourselves or if you have left it too late to obtain an occasional permission, you can ask a local holder of a licence to obtain an occasional licence for your function. If the local licensee is a member of your organisation he or she may be prepared to run the bar and donate the profits or a proportion of them to the cause. If not, it may still be worth providing a bar in order to increase the profits on ticket sales etc. The licensee will prefer to have plenty of time to obtain an occasional licence. If he or she gives a clear month's notice in writing no court attendance will be required unless the police make an objection to the grant. However, if he or she is willing to apply to the court in person, the only time requirement is that he should notify the chief officer of police 24 hours before the date of application.

A local licensee will need the following details to include in his application for an occasional licence:

1. the place and occasion for which the licence is required

2. the period for which it is required to be in force

3. the hours required to be specified in it

The occasional licence will specify the place, the period during which it is in force and the permitted hours.

5
ENTERTAINMENTS

If you are organising a fundraising entertainment you should ensure that you are not using any material that is subject to copyright, or that if you are, you have obtained the necessary permission for its use. You will also have to consider whether your entertainment requires a licence. In general (but see film shows, page 27) entertainments that are provided purely for members of a group and their guests will not require a licence from the local authority. But if your entertainment is to be open to the public a licence is necessary. It is an offence under each of the following acts for anyone to organise an entertainment without obtaining the necessary licence.

Plays

A public performance of a play requires a theatre licence. *Theatres Act 1968* s. 12

This can be obtained from the licensing authorities which are:
1. The London borough councils
2. The Common Council of the City of London
3. The District Council.
Where public performances are to be on one or two days only an occasional theatre licence can be granted on 14 days' notice to the licensing authority. A full theatre licence will require 21 days' notice to both the licensing authority and the police. In practice you need to give notice of application well outside these limits to ensure that you obtain your licence.

A theatre licence permits the sale of intoxicating liquor without a justices' licence provided that notice of the intention to sell intoxicating liquor is given to the clerk of the licensing justices. However, the local authority may refuse to grant a theatre licence without an undertaking from the promoter that intoxicating liquor will not be sold.

A theatre licence covers the provision of incidental music and dancing, or music and dancing that is part of a performance, so there is no need for an additional music and

dancing licence to cover this. It is an offence under the *Theatre Act* to present or direct a play which is obscene, likely to stir up racial hatred or to provoke a breach of the peace.

Music and dancing

A licence is required for public dancing or music or 'any other public entertainment of the like kind'. This is so whether the members of the public are participants or audience. The provisions relating to music and dancing licences differ slightly between Greater London and the rest of the country.

Greater London
The provisions for Greater London can be found in the *London Government Act 1963*, s. 52 and Schedule 12 (as amended by *Local Government Act 1985*, s. 16 Schedule 8). Application for a music and dancing licence should be made to the London borough council. If the application is for an occasional licence (i.e. for one or more particular occasions) 14 days' notice is required. A full licence requires 21 days' notice to the council, the police and the fire authority. In practice you need to give notice of application well outside these limits to ensure that you obtain your licence.

No fee can be charged for a music-and-dancing licence where the council is of the opinion that the entertainment is of an educational or other like character or is given for a charitable or other like purpose.

Outside Greater London
Here the governing Act is the *Local Government (Miscellaneous Provisions) Act 1982* Schedule 1. Application for a music and dancing licence should be made to the local district council. All applications including one for an occasional licence (i.e. for one or more occasions only) require 28 days' notice to the district council, the chief officer of police and to the fire authority. Once again, in practice you need to give notice well outside these limits to ensure

obtaining a licence.

A fee may not be charged for a music-and-dancing licence where the entertainment is to be in a church hall, a village hall or other similar building. The district council also have a discretion to make no charge or a reduced charge where the entertainment in question is of an educational character or given for a charitable or other like purpose.

It is not necessary to get a licence for a public entertainment outside Greater London where:

1. the music is incidental to a religious meeting or service

or

2. generally where the public entertainment takes place wholly or mainly in the open air

However, if you are planning a public musical entertainment (e.g. a pop festival) wholly or mainly in the open air on private land, you should check whether your district council has exercised its option to require licences for these. If they have passed such a resolution you will need a licence, which may impose conditions and restrictions for the sake of safety, hygiene and preventing unreasonable noise to neighbours.

Film shows

Premises used for a film exhibition require a licence. *Cinemas Act 1985.* This applies to video shows as well although not to simultaneous relaying of television broadcasts. An occasional film show will not require a licence provided the premises are not used for showing films on more than six days a year. It is still necessary, however, to give 7 days' notice of intention to use the premises for a film exhibition to the licensing authority (i.e. London borough council or district council), the fire authority and chief officer of police. The current regulations for film exhibitions must also be complied with together with any other conditions imposed and notified in writing

by the licensing authority. (The licensing authority will normally supply copies of the regulations.)

A licence to show films obtained in one district in respect of a 'moveable structure' (caravan etc) will allow the occupier to show films in another district provided two days' notice is given to the licensing authority, the fire authority and the chief of police. Where the show is wholly or mainly for children notice to the appropriate authorities is not sufficient, however, for occasional shows or shows in licensed moveable structures – theactual consent of the licensing authority must be obtained.

The *Cinemas Act* exceptionally requires licences for all film exhibitions whether open to the public or not. It then provides certain exemptions. These include the occasional exhibitions and exhibitions in moveable structures dealt with above, exhibitions given by certain organisations exempted by the Secretary of State and, of particular interest to small voluntary organisations, exhibitions given in a private dwelling house to which the public are not admitted, where the exhibition is not promoted for private gain. It follows that where a film show although confined to members of a group and their guests is not given in a private dwelling house but in a school, hired hall, etc., either a licence must be obtained or notice of an occasional exhibition must be given.

Sporting contests and exhibitions

The law relating to public sporting contests differs slightly between Greater London and the rest of the country.

Greater London
A licence is required for a public boxing or wrestling entertainment, *London Government Act 1963* Schedule 12 s. 4 as amended by *Local Government Act 1985*, save in certain cases including an entertainment provided by a school or by a bona fide association, club, hospital or

society not carried on for profit. The licensing authority is the London borough council. An occasional sports licence can be obtained on 14 days' notice to the council and the fire authority (a full sports licence requires 21 days' notice to the council, fire authority and police).

Outside Greater London
A licence is required for a public contest, exhibition or display of boxing, wrestling, judo, karate or similar sport, save where it takes place wholly or mainly in the open air. The licensing authority is the local district council. Twenty-eight days' notice to the council, the chief of police and the fire authority is necessary before a licence can be granted.

6
FUNDRAISING WITH MINORS

Children and young people under 18 can be enthusiastic fundraisers, but anyone running a project involving them should be aware of the extra legal responsibilities involved. People in charge of such a project stand *in loco parentis*, that is, they take on parental responsibilities to the children concerned. While children are under their control they must ensure the care and supervision that a reasonable parent would provide. If failure to meet this standard leads to injury or damage, those in charge may be held liable whether the injury was caused to the child or young person in question or caused by them to anyone else. Projects where children are involved therefore need careful planning and full insurance cover should be provided.

In addition, children and young people are specifically excluded from taking part in certain fundraising activities. The age restrictions imposed in the fundraising activities covered in this book are summarised below.

Collections

When house-to-house collections are undertaken under Home Office exemption or under licence, collectors may not be under 16. There is no such restriction where the collection is undertaken with the authority of a police certificate.

Local regulations for street collections usually impose a similar restriction but it is necessary to refer directly to the regulations in question. Ask at your town hall. There may be special provision for 14- to 16-year-olds.

Fêtes, bazaars etc.

Where lotteries and gaming take place under the provisions relating to exempt or non-commercial entertainments (see pages 8-9), there are no age restrictions on participants. So a child and young person may both sell and buy tickets at a small lottery, take part in amusements with prizes under s. 15 of the *Lotteries and Amusements Act 1976*, or use gaming machines provided under s. 33 of the *Gaming Act 1968*.

Lotteries

Tickets in societies' lotteries may not be sold by or to persons under 16. There are no restrictions on the age of participants in small or private lotteries.

Gaming

Where a members' club has been registered for gaming, no person under 18 may be present while the gaming takes place unless the gaming is bingo when they may be present but are not permitted to play.

Children and young people may take part in gaming at non-commercial entertainments under s. 15 of the *Lotteries and Amusements Act 1976*. They may also take part in gaming organised within the provisions of s. 40 of the *Gaming Act 1968* (bingo, bridge or whist drives in a club) or s. 41 (bingo, bridge or whist drives at an entertainment not for private gain).

Registration of a club for gaming by means of gaming machines will be refused or revoked where the premises are wholly or mainly used by persons under 18.

Intoxicating liquor

Registered clubs
Persons under 18 can be present on club premises which are registered for the supply of intoxicating liquor. There is no general prohibition on the supply of alcohol to minors in registered clubs but club rules together with conditions imposed by the justices may restrict this.

Occasional permissions

Where alcohol is served under the authority of an occasional permission persons under 18 may neither buy, sell or serve it. It is an offence for the holder of an occasional permission knowingly to permit contraventions of those rules.

Occasional licences

The law relating to licensed premises applies where an occasional licence is in force. This prohibits sale or consumption of alcohol by a person under 18, as well as their employment (whether for wages or not) in a bar while it is serving alcohol. Sections 169 and 170 of the *Licensing Act 1964* provide a number of offences relating to contravention of these rules of which the licensee or those employed by him could be held guilty.

Entertainments

Film shows

Where a film show is an occasional film show or in a licensed moveable structure, for example a caravan, it is generally sufficient to notify the local authority that it is to take place.

Where the show is wholly or mainly for children you must have the actual consent of the local authority to such shows.

In addition to Cinema Safety Regulations there are Regulations specifically relating to the attendance of children at film shows. The *Cinematograph (Children) No. 2* Regulations 1955 provide for children to be accompanied by someone over 16 in certain circumstances and for attendants to be present.

Entertainments where audiences exceed 100

If an entertainment involves audiences in excess of one hundred children the organiser must comply with the safety requirements of s 12 of the *Children and Young Persons Act 1933*. These require the organiser to provide sufficient number of adult attendants stationed where necesary and properly instructed to

1 prevent more children or other persons from entering the building than can be properly accommodated
2 control the movement of children and others entering and leaving the building
3 take all other reasonable precautions for the safety of the children

Child performers

Where a person under sixteen is to be involved in more than three public performances within six months a licence will be required from the local authority. There is an exception for performances arranged by a school, a body approved by the Secretary of State or a local authority where no payment is charged *(Children and Young Persons Act 1963)*.

7
SPONSORED EVENTS

Sponsored walks, runs, swims, etc have recently featured largely in fundraising activities. There is no legislation specifically dealing with such events but the fundraiser should bear in mind the general risk of civil liability referred to in the introduction together with the additional responsibility where children are involved.

If an event is to take place on a public highway, care must be taken not to cause obstruction. Consultation with the local police is a sensible precaution.

Difficulty arises surprisingly often in collecting sponsored money. As a matter of precaution the sponsorship form should allow sponsors to indicate the maximum sum recoverable so the amount in question does not take them by surprise. There could be problems in the recovery of sponsored money through the courts although generally it is not a debt that is likely to be pursued in this way.

Car-boot sales

If you intend to hold a car-boot sale you must consider whether it is necessary for you to give notice of your intention to the local authority. You should enquire whether your district or London borough council has passed a resolution applying s. 37 of the *Local Government (Miscellaneous Provisions) Act 1982* to the area. This section requires that notice must be given of any 'temporary market' not in a building or highway and with 5 or more stalls, vehicles, pitches etc.

Notice is *not* necessary where the proceeds of the market are applied solely or principally for charitable, social, sporting or political purposes. This exception allows garden fêtes, bazaars, etc to be held without notice.

However, most car-boot sales, even if run for such purposes, make their profit from the payments made by car owners or stall holders. The car owners or stall holders are attracted to the sale in the belief that their private profit will exceed the payment made, sometimes by a great deal. The proceeds of the market cannot then be said to be solely or principally for charitable, social, sporting or political purposes, and so notice will be necessary.

Such notice must include:

1. The full name and address of the person holding the market.

2. The day or days on which the market will be held and proposed opening and closing hours.

3. The site on which it is proposed it shall be held.

4. The name and address of the occupier of the site if he is not the person intending to hold the market.

The notice must be given not less than one month before the date on which it is proposed to hold the market. A person who holds a market or permits his land to be used as a temporary market without such notice is guilty of an offence. There is no other provision for example as to permission from the local authority. Once notice has been given the car-boot sale may go ahead as planned.

APPENDIX

A NOTE FOR CHARITIES THAT ARE CONSIDERING ENGAGING THE SERVICES OF A FUNDRAISING CONSULTANT OR FUNDRAISER

From *Malpractice in Fundraising for Charity: an NCVO Working Party Report* (See para.5.7 in the report. Note also that this appendix will need revision in the light of any legislation that may subsequently be enacted).

Preliminaries

1. It is assumed that you have considered and rejected the alternative of appointing an additional member of your own staff, full-time or part-time, to undertake the responsibilities that you have in mind.

2. You should be clear which of the following kinds of practitioner you are seeking to engage:

(a) a consultant, who will not engage in fundraising on your behalf but will advise you and will train your staff in the relevant operations;

(b) a fundraiser, who will personally undertake those operations on your behalf; or

(c) a co-venturer, who will undertake the sale of goods or services (eg the sale of tickets to an entertainment), some of the profits of which will accrue to your charity, and the remainder to him or his company.

3. Consult other charities known to you that have engaged recently in the kind of operation that you have in mind, and on a comparable scale. Ask whom they engaged; ask whether they were satisfied with the service that they received (if not, what went wrong?) and whether they would do the same again.

4. If that is not possible, consult the Local Development Unit at the National Council for Voluntary Organisations, 26 Bedford Square, London WC1B 3HU and obtain from the Institute of Charity Fundraising Managers, at 208 Market Towers, London SW8 5NQ (tel. 01-627 3436), a list of its members.

Considering the short list

5. Draw up in the light of these consultations a short list of possibles; ask them to indicate

(a) their relevant qualifications and experience;

(b) whether they are willing to work for you;

(c) how soon they will be available;

(d) how much time they will expect to give you and over what period it will be spread;

(e) what they estimate they their charges will be, how those charges will be calculated, and at what intervals they will expect to be paid;

(f) what reimbursement of expenses they will call for, what is their estimate of those expenses, and how they will be controlled (such control should be in your hands);

(g) what view they take of your target, and how much they would expect to raise for you, or help you to raise;

(h) the names of other charities for which they have recently worked, and to which you may refer (never take a practitioner's word for it that the service rendered to those charities was satisfactory; ask the charities themselves);

(j) whether they have a standard form of contract; if so, ask for a copy and study it carefully;

(k) what provision will be made for the premature termination of the contract by either party, and for the discharge of outstanding obligations after such termination.

6. Consider their responses (bearing in mind that, if they know what they are about, they will have read the document that you are now reading). They should ask to see you for discussion. How searching are the questions that they put to you? Do they fully appreciate the strengths and weaknesses of your position? Remember that the best adviser may be the one who sees most clearly the difficulties to be overcome rather than the one who appears to share your own enthusiasm for your work.

7. Examine with care and in sufficient detail how they arrive at their estimates of the sums that they expect to raise, of the time that they expect to spend on the job, and of their expenses. Are the estimates realistic?

8. Discuss with them how, if you engage them, they will set about the work. What will they actually do, and when? What methods will they employ (those methods, and any change in them should require your approval)?

9. If the operation of a lottery is proposed, make sure that the arrangements will be within the law (you may refer to *But Is It Legal? Fundraising and the Law* (Bedford Square Press, 1988).

10. Discuss with them the volume of other work they have in hand: will there be enough time left for you? Once you are committed to them is there a risk that they will take on so much other work that they cannot do you justice?

11. What staff will be employed on your work? You must have an opportunity of meeting them before you are committed.

12. Be particularly careful with any who propose that you should pay them a commission on takings as a basis for their remuneration. The Charity Comissioners and others (including the NCVO Working Party) advise against it, and it has been associated with malpractice. It will probably be better to find someone who charges on a time basis. If nevertheless, in spite of this advice, you do agree to the commission basis of remuneration, make clear that you will expect donors to be told what percentage of their gifts will be retained by the practitioner; indeed this is probably required by law. See also that it is clear that the percentage will be charged only on relevant gifts — it would be inappropriate that it should be chargeable on a legacy (where the will may well have been made long before the FRP was associated with you), or on a government grant.

Negotiation with the candidate of your choice

13. Ensure that you will have adequate control over the methods of fundraising to be used and that they will not be such as to bring your charity into disrepute. Make sure that no-one in the practitioner's organisation will be allowed to claim, expressly or by implication, to be an employee of your charity.

14. Make sure that donors will be asked to make cheques payable to the charity, not to the FRP, and that any contributions that he may receive in cash will be paid into the bank, with the least possible delay, for the credit of your charity. Do not agree to any arrangement whereby he may deduct remuneration or expenses from receipts.

15. Take up a banker's reference.

16. Ask whether the practitioner has ever been bankrupt, or has been a director of any company that has gone into liquidation. Will the contract be with the practitioner personally or with a company? If the latter, will the practitioner personally guarantee

the company's observance of its obligations? If the sums involved may be substantial, consider making a status enquiry through Dun & Bradstreet Ltd or a similar organisation.

17. Make sure that the practitioner will not be able without your express prior agreement in writing to incur obligations on your behalf, and that any money that may be handled on your behalf reaches you quickly enough to avoid risk of being used or attached to meet obligations of the practitioner or anyone else concerned. Consider whether the circumstances (incuding the sums at risk) make it appropriate for you to ask for a bond, fidelity insurance policy, or the like.

18. Make sure that information obtained from you, or information obtained by the practitioner from other sources while working for you, will be your property, and that other clients will not be allowed to have the benefit of it without your consent.

19. When you have made your choice, you should insist on a written contract. Make sure that you do not get committed unwittingly before that stage is reached. It may be wise to mark preliminary letters 'Subject to Contract'.

20. Make sure that the contract correctly reflects all that has been agreed with you in preliminary discussion. Once there is a written contract, it alone may bind the practitioner and informal understandings, or even letters that have passed between you, cannot be relied upon.

FURTHER READING

Patersons Licensing Acts, N. Martin (96th edition, 1988)

Gaming, Lotteries, Fund Raising and the Law, Jarlath Finney (Sweet and Maxwell, 1982)

The Licensing Guide, Michael Underhill (Longman, 9th edition, 1985)

Licensing Practice and Procedure, Kenneth W. Pain (Fourmat, 2nd edition, 1986)

Malpractice in Fundraising for Charity: an NCVO Working Party Report, 1986. Available from NCVO Appeals Department.

Bars, Charities and the Law, National Federation of Community Organisations, 1982.

INDEX

alcohol, consumption of and minors 31
amusements with prizes, rules for 9

bars,
    licensing of 22-24
    running of 22-24
        on club premises 22-23
bars at fundraising functions,
    applications for licensing of 23-24
    permission needed for 23
    running of 23
Betting, Gaming and Lotteries Act (1963) 11
Betting and Gaming Duties Act (1981) 19
bingo, rules for 14-15
bingo duty 19
bridge drives, rules for 14-15

car-boot sales, local authority requirements
        for notice of 28
charitable purposes, definition of 4
Children and Young Persons Act (1933) 31
                                  (1963) 31
Cinemas Act 31,   (1985) 27
club premises,
    conditions for registration of 22
    grounds for refusal of registration of 22
    registration of for sale of alcohol 22
clubs,
    refusal of registration of 16
    registered,
        minors in 30
        rules for sale of alcohol at 23
collecting boxes in premises 6
collections,
    definition of 4
    house-to-house see house-to-house
        collections
    street see street collections
copyright material 26
corporation tax 2

damage, liability for 1, 34

entertainments,
    exempt from Lotteries and
        Amusements Act 8, 9
    licensing of 26-28
    musical, open air 27
    non-commercial 8, 9
events, sponsored see sponsored events

film shows,
    licensing of, exemptions from 27
    licensing of premises used for 27
    regulations for 27
film shows for children, local authority
        consent for 31
fire authorities, notice required by 26, 27, 28
fundraising with minors 30-31
    extra responsibilities of 30
    insurance cover for 30
    restrictions on 30
fundraisers,
    professional 2
        payment of 2
        terms of employment of 2
fundraising,
    legal regulation of 1
    pitfalls of 1
fundraising activities,
    expert advice on 1
    insurance of 1

games, prohibited by Gaming Act 14
gaming,
    definition of 8
    equal chance 14
    excise duty on 19
    and minors 30
    permitted 14-18
    restrictions on 14

Gaming Act (1968) 8, 9, 12, 14, 15, 16, 17, 18, 30
  general rules of 14
Gaming Board,
  lotteries registered with 13
  returns of lotteries to 13
gaming machines 17-19
  Gaming Act rules for 17, 18
  hire of 9
  licensing authorities for 17
  licensing of under Gaming Act 18
  local restrictions on 17
  permits for 17
  prizes given by 18
  refusal of licences for 18
  rules for use of 9
  use of on premises registered under
    Gaming Act 18-19
gaming premises, registered, rules for 16-17
gaming with prizes machines, rules for 17-18
garden fêtes, legal provisions for 8

house-to-house collections 4
  collectors, duties of 5
  duties of promoters of 5
  licences for, reasons for refusal of 5
  licensing authorities for 4
  licensing of 2
    Home Office Exemption from 4
  police certificates for 4
House-to-House Collections Act (1939) 4
House-to-House Collections Regulations
    (1947) 4, 5

injuries, liability for 1

law, reasons for complying with vi
licences,
  occasional 23, 24
    obtaining of by licensees 24
    rules for 23, 24
    timing of applications for 24
Licensing Act (1964) 22
Licensing (Occasional Permissions)
    Act (1933) 23
local authorities, returns of lotteries to 13
Local Government Act (1963) 26, 27
                    (1985) 26, 27
Local Government (Miscellaneous
    Provisions) Act (1982) 26, 28
lotteries,
  allowable expenses for 12, 13

definition of 8, 10-14
medium-term, rules for 13
private 10
  promotion of by individuals 10
registration of, reasons for refusal of 13
rules for 10-14
rules for proceeds of 12
short-term, rules for 13
small, rules for 8-9
Lotteries and Amusements Act
    (1976) 8, 9, 10, 11, 12, 14, 30
Lotteries Regulations (1977) 11, 12
lottery prizes 12

machines, gaming see gaming machines
members' clubs,
  definition of 15
  registration of 15-16
miners' welfare institutes,
  definition of 15
  registration of 15-16
minors, regulations concerning
    5, 14, 27, 30, 31
money, rules for collecting of 5, 6
music and dancing,
  licences for,
    in Greater London 26
    outside Greater London 26-27

plays, licensing of public performances of 26
police, notice required by 26, 27, 28
Police Factories (Miscellaneous Provisions)
    Act (1916) 5
premises,
  registration of 15-16
  objections to 16
prizes, rules for 8, 9
proceeds, rules for 8, 9

societies, registration of 11
societies' lotteries 10-13
  benefits of 10, 11
  checklist for 14
  permissible purposes of 11
  registration of 11-12
societies' lottery schemes, rules for 11, 12
sponsored events 34
  on public highways 34
sponsored money, collection of 34
sporting contests,
  licensing of,

in Greater London 27-28
outside Greater London 28
Street Collection (Metropolitan Police
District) Regulations (1979) 6
street collections 5-6
licensing authorities for 6
timing of applications for 6
sweepstakes, office 10

theatre licences,
entertainments covered by 26
occasional 26

VAT 2

whist drives, rules for 14-15

Other titles in the Practical Guides series:

Employing People in Voluntary Organisations
Finding and Running Premises
Getting into Print: An introduction to publishing
Government Grants: A guide for voluntary organisations
Opening the Town Hall Door: An introduction to local government
Organising Your Finances: A guide to good practice
Starting a Voluntary Agency: The legal choices
Voluntary Organisations and New Technology
Working Effectively: A guide to evaluation techniques
You Are The Governor: How to be effective in your local school

Printed in Great Britain
by Amazon